Communication

How To Have Fun In Conversations, Increase Your
Assertiveness, And Have Wonderful Interactions For
Meaningful Relationships Is A Guide To Effective
Communication Skills

Friedrich Suppan

TABLE OF CONTENT

Several Additional Factors That Can Contribute To A Diminished Self-Perception 1

The Development Of Timing Programmes 27

Putting Together Your Message 52

When Conducted In Person 100

Strategies For Cultivating Assertiveness On An Individual Level 122

Several Additional Factors That Can Contribute To A Diminished Self-Perception

One adverse consequence of bullying is the erosion of a child's self-assurance, contributing to the formation of a negative self-perception. This impression is exceedingly difficult to dislodge, as it becomes firmly embedded in the child's psyche throughout the course of several years. An inadequate self-perception hinders the acquisition of new knowledge.

Tragic Childhood Experiences

Occasionally, children may encounter the unfortunate circumstance of losing a profoundly significant individual in their lives, someone who has consistently served as their unwavering source of guidance. Consequently, they may recoil into a self-protective enclosure, harboring apprehensions that others will inevitably fall short in delivering the same level of care, affection, and encouragement. They never make an attempt to personally ascertain whether the state of the world is satisfactory or not.

Threatened Childhood

Individuals who have experienced a tumultuous upbringing characterized by excessive violence and an ongoing fight for survival have the capability to internalize their survival instincts as well. They are unable to find the sanctuary they have diligently sought, leading them to turn inward.

Abuse

The provision of physical, psychological, sexual, or emotional harm to a child can engender feelings of insecurity and lead to the development of a solitary demeanor in said individual. These instances of mistreatment yield significant detrimental consequences and leave a lasting imprint on the psychological well-being of the child. These children cease to place complete reliance and belief in others, while concurrently developing trust-related concerns.

They have the propensity to develop introverted tendencies and isolate themselves from others. It may present a considerable challenge to instruct them in social skills due to their profound deficit in trust, surpassing mere deficiencies in social skills. They are apprehensive about embracing this particular realm.

General body postures

Emotions can similarly be discerned through the analysis of bodily stances. Based on empirical research, it has been observed that the ability to recognize emotions is enhanced when contrasting the body posture with that of a distinct or neutral emotion. For example, an individual who is experiencing anger will demonstrate dominance over others and maintain a stance that is open to approach. In contradistinction to an enraged individual, an individual who experiences fear would exhibit characteristics of vulnerability and submissiveness, with evident avoidance inclinations reflected in their posture.

The posture or positioning of an individual occasionally serves as an indicator of their emotions. An individual who exhibits ease, receptiveness, and a general willingness to listen assumes a still position in the rear of their seat, inclines forward, and acknowledges the conversation through subtle affirmations. Conversely, an individual who maintains a crossed leg and arms at rest while actively tapping their foot indicates impatience and a lack of emotional involvement in the dialogue.

During a conversational setting, when an individual keeps their arms positioned by their sides and directs their feet towards the speaker, it is indicative of their attentiveness and active participation in the ongoing dialogue. Even the slightest alteration to this stance could yield momentous effects. In the context of Balinese customs, it is deemed discourteous to position oneself with elevated arms.

The task of positioning the package requires flexing the elbows inward and relocating the hands either equipped with or without fingers onto the belt or trousers. In contrast, the superman stance necessitates positioning both hands or fists in close proximity to the hips or lower back.

An individual can exhibit signs of rigidity or tension if they have sustained a consistent bodily posture over a prolonged duration. By intermittently adjusting their position, even if only marginally, individuals can mitigate this phenomenon.

Chest specifically

The stance and mobility of the thorax play a pivotal role in determining the overall signals emitted by the entire body. Broadly speaking, the comparative expansion or contraction of the thorax, particularly in the vicinity of the sternum, serves as a crucial determinant of both temperament and disposition. In everyday situations, when evaluating the body language of the chest, a spontaneous evaluation of these aspects pertaining to shape and volume takes place.

When the chest exhibits a more pronounced and anteriorly-positioned posture, it serves as an indicator of one's confidence. If one's posture exhibits a noticeable projection forward, it could suggest a desire to attain social prominence and express a sense of physical assurance. A retracted chest can serve as an indicator of diminished confidence.

When an individual shifts their chest in proximity to someone else, it can indicate heightened focus on that person during a conversation, or, on certain occasions, it might signify assertiveness or aggression.

The act of placing one's hand on the chest can convey multiple implications. An individual who places both hands upon their heart could be displaying this gesture as a means to underscore their sincerity in verbal communication. Applying pressure to the chest area, particularly in the vicinity of the heart, may indicate physical unease, potentially arising from heightened stress and tension. Similar to other instances of chest body language, this behavior might be correlated with an individual's heart rate.

1. Familiarize yourself with the other person's sensitive points.

Certain words and phrases possess the potential to give rise to a multitude of misunderstandings. Within the professional setting, it is possible that you may be characterized as excessively amicable, an attribute that may not necessarily bear a favorable connotation. It may suggest that you possess a lenient approach towards others, have difficulty in effectively delegating tasks, or struggle to enforce accountability. This implies that whenever individuals label you as excessively kind, you can interpret it similarly to how your colleagues perceive it. Perhaps, there might be someone else who is recognized for being excessively kind in a similar manner within their professional capacity, and when this individual is labeled as excessively kind, they may not view it as a particularly flattering comment.

Familiarize yourself with the other individual's sensitivities to prevent inadvertent consternation over benign matters.

2. Rephrase

This principle is applicable in both the avoidance of misinterpretation and the prevention of any potential misunderstandings with the other party. In instances where an individual's statement lacks clarity or there is an indication that your message is not clearly understood by the recipient, simply proceed by restating the information provided. Allow me to clarify my intention by stating that what I intended to convey is so and so. Is the matter comprehensible, or would you require further elucidation? Observe whether they are expressing their acknowledgment of your statements through both verbal and nonverbal cues.

If it appears that the individual is unreceptive to the message you are attempting to convey, indicated by nonverbal signals such as crossing of the arms and legs or fidgeting, it is advisable to promptly discontinue the current topic of discussion and shift the conversation to a different subject in order to encourage them to become more receptive. Once they demonstrate a heightened level of receptivity and appear more open and at ease (taking into consideration their non-verbal cues), reintroduce the challenging subject matter. The objective is to induce them into a state of mind that is more open and willing to receive information.

The individual ought to exhibit a heightened subconscious receptiveness towards considering your perspective and placing trust in your words. Do not revert to discussing the initial subject until you have successfully redirected their attention to this standpoint.

3. Assess an Individual's Comprehension Level

Irrespective of whether you are engaging with a substantial gathering or conversing with an individual, it is advisable to ascertain their fundamental comprehension prior to embarking on a discourse laden with specialized terminology and intricate concepts. These terminologies or technical terms can lead to significant misunderstandings if the individual lacks familiarity with them.

On occasion, it is possible to presume that the individual possesses a thorough understanding of specific terminology and expressions, and consequently employ them without restraint during the discourse. However, it may later come to your attention that the person has ascribed a completely distinct interpretation to the information conveyed. The decoder must comprehend your statement within the appropriate context. Attempt to engage in a meaningful exchange or engage in casual conversation as a means to assess the individual's degree of comprehension.

4. Refrain from crafting excessively lengthy sentences

Please streamline your message by using concise and persuasive sentences. The greater the extent to which you make them long-winded and verbose, the diminished their impact will become. Furthermore, by introducing complexity, there is a heightened probability of encountering misunderstandings. When employing concise vocabulary, phrases, and sentences, there is a greater likelihood of accurately understanding the intended message. Refrain from unnecessarily inflating or embellishing sentences. They could potentially forfeit their inherent significance.

5. Request the candid and unfiltered insights of a reliable confidant.

To gain insights into how you are perceived or how you come across to others, it would be beneficial to enlist the support of a reliable confidant. Kindly request them to be exceptionally candid in providing feedback regarding the impression you ultimately create. This individual must possess qualities of reliability and integrity, as well as the ability to provide authentic and constructive critiques. An individual who possesses a deep understanding of your character will be able to discern accurately in which areas others might assess you correctly and in which areas their judgments may be flawed. It could potentially be advantageous to ascertain the perceptions of society towards oneself and ascertain if it is worth the efforts involved. Allow your friend to engage in a simulated dialogue with you, during which they can identify distinct occasions where your thoughts are likely to be comprehended with clarity, as well as moments where miscommunications are more probable.

Tone

If you are inclined to engage in a substantial dialogue with your partner, it is probable that your emotional state is profoundly affected. It is permissible to express such emotion to your partner; however, it is advisable to exercise caution in modulating your vocal tone. Please ensure that you do not allow your voice to escalate to a level that may give the impression of yelling at them. Ensure that the tone you employ does not convey anger, especially if you are simply expressing enthusiasm or frustration about a particular matter.

The manner in which you speak will determine the direction the conversation takes. Should you adopt a tone characterized by frustration and anger, your partner will instinctively feel compelled to become defensive. This does not foster effective communication. Maintain a transparent and candid demeanor, appropriately exhibiting emotion when it enhances the delivery of your message, while ensuring a consistent and confident tone.

The higher your level of confidence in the subject matter you are discussing with your partner, the greater the likelihood that you will sustain a balanced and composed demeanor. Consider all potential reactions that your companion may express and strategize effective counterarguments. The greater sense of assurance you possess regarding your preparation, the more adeptly you will sustain a composed demeanor while effectively conveying your message.

Body Language

When engaging in a significant conversation with your spouse, it is crucial to ensure that you maintain receptivity to their input and response. Assuming an open and receptive posture by keeping your arms either to your sides or resting in your lap will facilitate a sense of comfort and signal your eagerness to receive their response. Your significant other is probably the person who possesses the deepest understanding of your personality, surpassing most individuals in perceiving and interpreting your nonverbal cues.

Active Listening

Active listening is arguably the utmost pivotal component of successful interpersonal communication. A large number of individuals engage in listening with the intention to respond, however, the suitable approach to proficient communication involves listening with the intention to comprehend. Attentively consider your spouse's responses and paraphrase the information to them.

For instance, if one comprehends that you harbor doubts about this particular plan, it is probable that you will confirm such uncertainty and possibly expatiate further on the underlying reasons. Should they have any doubts, they will take the opportunity to rectify any misunderstandings by elucidating their thoughts using an alternative approach. Engaging in active listening in this manner holds paramount significance in fostering effective communication within your interpersonal connections.

At present, we may temporarily dismiss the inconsistencies between the language employed for sales purposes and the divergences in the objective and approach of the lecture. We will now proceed to analyze a hypothetical situation in which individuals need to exercise caution regarding persuasive techniques employed to promote sales, gain endorsement for a political agenda or candidate, or influence compliance with managerial directives pertaining to business practices. In an analogous manner, when faced with a contrasting scenario, we shall delve into the imperative for listeners to demonstrate a combination of receptivity and discernment. They should be poised to acquire knowledge rather than display resistance or apathy towards the teachings presented. Nevertheless, they ought to exercise discernment by not accepting unquestioningly everything that is imparted to them. It is widely acknowledged that the act of listening holds great significance. Furthermore, it is widely recognized that among the four components encompassing verbal communication, namely writing, reading, speaking, and listening, the latter is often inadequately executed.

It is undeniable that individuals, upon careful consideration, would not hesitate to acknowledge that the proficiency they have attained in writing, reading, and speaking far surpasses, if not outweighs, their competence in listening. When pressed for a reason, it is plausible to propose that his education included writing instruction, alongside some degree of emphasis on enhancing reading and verbal communication skills, albeit to a notably lesser extent (to an extent that is both striking and unexpected). The level of consideration given to listening ability was exceedingly minimal.

An alternative perspective could be offered by the individual who holds the mistaken notion that listening consists merely of maintaining silence while the other party is talking. While possessing good manners is imperative, minimal talent is necessary.

We express immense gratitude to the esteemed American enterprise, Sperry, for their diligent endeavors in combating the pervasive apathy and lack of knowledge surrounding hearing impairment through their admirable initiatives encompassing both advertising campaigns and informative literature. Furthermore, Sperry has allocated corporate resources and dedicated efforts towards the creation and implementation of comprehensive listening courses, which are accessible to all staff members regardless of their position. This initiative is driven by Sperry's recognition that shortcomings in effective listening and the consequent breakdown of communication represent significant impediments that lead to unproductive time utilization, inefficiencies in operations, compromised strategies, and unsatisfactory decision-making across all sectors of the corporation's business endeavors.

Based on one of Sperry's pamphlets, it is asserted that listening is prioritized during the initial stages of brain development, constituting one of the four fundamental acts in the process of communication. Adolescent, commonly utilized in everyday contexts (46 percent of instances), yet largely omitted from educational curriculum throughout all levels of schooling.

Conversely, in the sequential progression of development, speaking is acquired subsequent to listening, it is employed approximately 30% of the time, and its instruction in educational institutions is nearly as lacking as that of listening. "Reading is acquired prior to writing; it is practiced with greater frequency compared to writing (15 percent vs. Furthermore, writing instruction is not as extensive as that received for other subjects, with a mere 9 percent allocation.

Irrespective of the acceptance of these facts and numerical figures, it is evident that the speaking and listening skills of the general populace are considerably less developed than their writing and reading abilities. Despite the considerable shortcomings displayed by our typical high school and college graduates in writing and reading, their deficiencies in these fundamental skills cannot be emphasized enough. However, it is in the realm of speaking that their performance becomes even more abysmal, with listening being the most severely impacted.

The aforementioned Sperry pamphlet delineates numerous inappropriate behaviors that impede or compromise effective listening. One additional manner in which people demonstrate poor listening skills is by placing excessive emphasis on the speaker's mannerisms of speech rather than the actual content being conveyed. Another manifestation of this is when individuals feign engagement with the speaker, while quietly allowing their thoughts to drift towards unrelated matters. Additionally, distractions of all kinds can divert one's attention away from the speaker and the message being delivered. Furthermore, individuals may overreact to certain words or phrases that elicit negative emotional responses. The aforementioned Sperry booklet subsequently presents a set of "ten keys to successful listening" in order to counteract these detrimental tendencies, which we have likely observed in others if not in ourselves. A considerable portion of these recommendations simply consist of mandates to overcome or eliminate the aforementioned unfavourable practices that hinder effective listening.

The Development Of Timing Programmes

The essential supplies required for this activity encompass paper, paper sheets, and various coloring implements.

A required minimum of 20 to 25 individuals.

Duration: Approximately 30 minutes.

The implementation of regulations and structured schedules holds significant value when it comes to fostering a supportive environment for individuals with AS in the younger age group. This practice entails maintaining a systematic documentation of upcoming events, thereby mitigating the levels of stress and anxiety experienced by such individuals.

Organizing people in groups. Every individual is directed to carefully record the tasks they carry out on a daily basis, arranging them in order of importance.

After elucidating and executing the initial phase, the subsequent focus lies on articulating the significance of systematically arranging the tasks undertaken on a daily basis, thereby ensuring comprehensiveness in their execution without any omissions.

Orientation sessions are conducted to provide detailed explanations of schedules, which can be represented in tabular format, systematically organizing each event in order of significance and allotted time. They may be accompanied by illustrations or visuals that enhance their appeal and aesthetic charm.

Upon the conclusion of the activity, there will be an opportunity to articulate the developed activity and share personal sentiments, thereby organizing and structuring the undertaken activities.

This game offers a sense of security to children and adolescents diagnosed with AS, as it alleviates their concerns about impending events and aids in their emotional regulation through the successful completion of each task.

CHAPTER EIGHT

Methods for Enhancing Communication Aptitude

If you perceive a deficiency in your core communication skills, there exist several efficacious methodologies to enhance them. Below are a few recommendations for improving your communication abilities:

Exert Endeavors to Engage in Active Listening

Proficient communicators consistently demonstrate a propensity for active listening. Active listening involves providing affirmative responses to others' statements and inquiring further to display attentiveness.

Enforce the significance of nonverbal communication. Acquiring comprehension of nonverbal cues and signals can aid in averting miscommunication and expressing interest to individuals in one's vicinity. When engaging with others within a professional framework, do ensure that you meticulously observe your facial expressions and nonverbal cues. The nonverbal signals you convey hold sway over the first impression you make. Sustaining visual contact, restraining gestural movements, and upholding correct bodily alignment all foster a favorable initial perception when encountering an individual for the first time.

Self-control Your Emotions

It is of utmost importance to exercise emotional management and express them in a suitable manner within the relevant context, primarily to foster effective communication and ensure one's personal welfare. Permitting excessive emotional involvement to permeate a professional setting can potentially lead to suboptimal communication and discord.

Solicit Feedback

There is no dishonor in proactively seeking frank feedback from colleagues with respect to your communication abilities. By soliciting input from colleagues or subordinates regarding strategies to enhance communication proficiency, you can enhance your comprehension of the impression you create within the professional arena. Foster a willingness to consider divergent perspectives and cultivate a motivation to enhance interpersonal relationships with colleagues.

Enhance Your Public Speaking Proficiency

Although the thought of public speaking may appear daunting, there is no superior method to enhance one's communication abilities than actively pursuing occasions to address an audience. Outstanding individuals with great communication skills possess the capacity to effectively articulate their emotions in a concise manner, regardless of whether they are addressing a vast gathering or engaging in a personal conversation. Regularly addressing a group will bring attention to your aptitudes and constraints, compelling you to cultivate robust communication practices.

Create a Filter

Proficient communicators generally exhibit elevated social prowess and possess the capacity to adapt their articulations of thoughts and emotions in consideration of the individuals in their vicinity. Demonstrate the ability to discern and effectively convey your thoughts and emotions in a diverse range of interpersonal circumstances. Constructing a filtering mechanism will serve to enhance existing communication competencies, aiding in the preservation of utmost decorum while mitigating potential tensions in professional encounters.

• OCD is Rare

When it comes to mental illnesses, obsessive-compulsive disorders rank among the most common. In the United States, it has been reported that the prevalence of Obsessive-Compulsive Disorder (OCD) is estimated to be one percent per population, with half of the cases classified as severe. Even in the region of West Africa, over 1 million cases of OCD (Obsessive-Compulsive Disorder) are diagnosed annually. In what manner, then, can it be considered anything other than a prevalent psychological ailment? Individuals suffering from OCD, along with other types of illnesses that face significant societal stigma, are prone to silence themselves about their condition due to the belief that discussing it is inconsequential or may result in severe judgment from others. In contrast to other medical ailments, Obsessive-Compulsive Disorder (OCD) can be more readily concealed. However, it exacts a significant toll on the individual and only exacerbates the condition. When individuals feign the absence of such compulsive thoughts in public, they must exert significantly more effort to alleviate their anxiety when they are in solitude. The majority are also commonly referred to as solitary individuals or individuals with introverted tendencies, which effectively conceals the underlying issue. Other individuals are perceived as peculiar because, in addition to consistently keeping to themselves, they occasionally exhibit compulsive behaviors that are unknown to those in their vicinity.

- This phenomenon is exclusively prevalent in families with hereditary or dysfunctional traits.

Some instances of Obsessive-Compulsive Disorder (OCD) are found to have a familial link, wherein one or more family members exhibit symptoms of OCD or other mental disorders upon thorough examination. However, it is important to note that this does not hold true for all cases. Frequently, incidences are documented in which no member of the family exhibits symptoms of a mental disorder. Genetics alone does not constitute the exclusive means through which an individual may acquire this disorder. Majority of the time, the problem is kick-started later in life by socially awkward or embarrassing situations. The occurrence in their lives is clung to and revisited repeatedly in a fervent quest for ways they could have executed it more effectively. It could equally be initiated by alternative factors. Therefore, a singular cause for OCD does not exist. It could initiate during early childhood, as exemplified in children diagnosed with OCD, as well as in advanced stages of adulthood. This misconception has served as a catalyst for the fragmentation of numerous familial units. When someone with OCD publicly discloses their condition, it is possible that other family members may gradually find themselves distancing from friends or partners due to the perception that the disorder is hereditary and they are unwilling to handle such circumstances. Additionally, there exists a fallacious notion that individuals grappling with compulsive disorders attribute the cause of their difficulties to a dysfunctional upbringing under inept parental guidance in an unstable household. However, the reality is that a considerable number of individuals diagnosed with OCD originate from content households, indeed. They benefit from exceptionally dedicated guardians and idyllic upbringing experiences. It is imperative to clearly emphasize that while genetics may have a role in specific cases, this is not predominantly the situation. There should be no social stigma attached to any type of mental illness, and individuals should not be left unsupported in managing their medical conditions in isolation.

Personalize your statements

Utilizing the use of "I" statements allows individuals to effectively express their thoughts or emotions without coming across as accusatory or menacing in nature. By way of illustration, one could express "I dissent" instead of "You are mistaken." In case you have a solicitation, kindly state "I would appreciate your assistance with this matter" rather than "You must do this." Such an approach deliberately shifts the emphasis from their actions to your own sentiments regarding the situation.

Using "I" statements can mitigate the impact of your statements and diminish the potency of your allegations by shifting the focus from attributing blame to acknowledging one's own perspective. This creates the perception that you are neither passing judgment nor but merely articulating the impact their actions have on you. Fundamentally, when commencing a sentence by employing the phrase "You...," it tends to be perceived as a form of criticism or an act of aggression, thus causing individuals to become guarded and defensive. When utilizing the pronoun "I", the emphasis shifts towards expressing personal emotions and the impact of their conduct on oneself. Moreover, it demonstrates a greater sense of responsibility for one's own responses, while reducing the tendency to assign blame. This approach aids in reducing the occurrence of defensiveness in the counterpart, exemplifying the act of assuming responsibility, and propelling both individuals towards constructive transformation. For example:

It is imperative that you cease that behavior immediately.

I would appreciate it if you refrained from engaging in such behavior.

When employed in the context of factual statements rather than subjective assessments or categorizations, this formula offers a straightforward, non-confrontational, and more accountable approach to conveying to individuals the impact their actions have on you. This method serves as an effective means of presenting your argument as it greatly minimizes potential counterarguments by rendering it difficult for others to dispute its validity. Concerning the matter at hand, it pertains to your emotions. One cannot cease experiencing one's emotions merely due to others perceiving them as incorrect.

To begin with, initiate the conduct, subsequently delineate the outcomes, and finally articulate the emotions. Presented below is the equation:

When one engages in [their behavior], it subsequently leads to [the outcomes of their behavior], thereby eliciting feelings of [your emotions].

Examples:

Upon your tardy arrival, I am compelled to endure a period of waiting, which elicits a sense of frustration within me.

When you grant permission to the children for something that I have previously prohibited, it diminishes certain aspects of my parental authority, leading me to feel weakened in my role.

Your loud vocalization causes me to experience a sense of being personally targeted.

Utilize straightforward and precise language. Please observe and assess your conduct throughout a day, and subsequently make an effort to integrate varying structures, as exemplified above, during your next endeavor.

Conflict Within Your Team

There will perpetually exist conflicts within your team. This can be attributed to varying individual personalities, divergent sets of priorities, disparities in comprehending the team or project objectives, or contrasting approaches to working and managing tasks. It is imperative to promptly attend to any emerging concerns, as failure to do so may impede the efficiency of the team's productivity. As an integral member of the team and, of greater significance, as an individual in a leadership role, it proves advantageous to possess the capacity to identify a potential conflict scenario and possess the requisite skills to effectively navigate and resolve it.

While conflict may yield detrimental effects on a team, it also possesses potential benefits when effectively managed. When a team encounters conflict, the ensuing resolution process affords them the opportunity to effectively navigate the discomfort and develop a renewed sense of mutual trust.

Team conflict typically arises due to multiple factors:

Conflict arising from divergent task responsibilities, characterized by incomplete adherence to one's assigned role within the team.

Leadership conflicts may arise due to divergent personalities that result in varying approaches to team management, leading to disagreements among individuals involved. Evaluating one's own leadership style is crucial in minimizing potential conflicts within the team.

Conflicts arising from divergent work styles are commonplace, as individuals exhibit their unique approaches to working, leading to disagreements caused by varying work paces.

The variances in personalities can foster a sense of competitiveness within the team, leading to the team members offering support to one another during arduous projects and intervening when a member encounters difficulties.

Conflict Prevention

Prevention entails exhibiting a consciousness of the factors that incite conflicts and employing a tactful approach to diminish or eliminate discord within your team. This entails the utilization of distinct strategies and activities that cater to the diverse composition of individuals comprising your team.

In order to mitigate the occurrence of conflicts, it is imperative to foster a culture of regular communication among your team members. Once your team develops a habit of effective communication, misunderstandings are swiftly addressed and tension is alleviated, thereby facilitating a more accurate comprehension of the predetermined project objectives. When the entire team cultivates attributes such as patience, adaptability, courtesy, impartiality, receptiveness, and coherence, instances of disagreements and misconceptions will be effectively thwarted.

It is imperative to approach team conflict with a constructive mindset and a keen sense of self-awareness, taking into consideration your emotional state. If you are experiencing anger, it is important to ensure that you have attained a state of calmness before addressing the issue. Otherwise, the ensuing discussion has the potential to escalate beyond control, leading to negative consequences for the team instead of positive outcomes. It is imperative that your attention remains fixated on the matter at hand and refrains from targeting any individual.

Energy Tools have the potential to enhance intuition and facilitate effective communication with animals.

I hold a firm conviction that the set of five uncomplicated exercises, which I refer to as my "Energy Tools," serve as the fundamental underpinning for all prosperous engagements in animal communication. The transformation I have witnessed among my students as they acquire these skills has been truly remarkable. By means of these instruments, accessing their intuition and establishing communication with animals becomes significantly more convenient and innate. Their intuitive capabilities are considerably more readily attainable.

During my tenure as an instructor for the Advanced Animal Communication Class, I had the privilege of educating not only those who had previously enrolled in my introductory course, but also those who had completed a foundational course with another educator. The majority of other instructors in animal communication neglect these particular exercises. However, upon learning my five Energy Tools, these advanced students experienced a significant leap in their animal communication outcomes. They frequently provide feedback acknowledging that my Energy Tools were the crucial factor enabling them to achieve consistent and readily available animal communication abilities.

The Daily Energy Practice Utilizing My Assortment of Five Energy Instruments

The Grounding Cord, Running Your Energy, Energizing Your Chakras, Center of Head, and the Golden Sun are the five Energy Tools that I impart during my teachings. Collectively, these uncomplicated exercises facilitate the flow of energy throughout all areas of your physique, establish a connection with the environment, and enable you to attain the centered, equanimous state that is imperative for triumph as a communicator with animals. The compilation of these five exercises constitutes my Daily Energy Routine. I have engaged in this particular practice on a daily basis for nearly fifteen years, and I actively advocate for my students to adopt this as a regular lifelong habit as well.

Consistent practice is essential as it engenders a progressive, accumulative impact of undertaking these exercises. Engaging in this daily routine enables the removal of energetic obstacles, the harmonization of your chakras, the cultivation of energy manipulation skills, and the advancement towards what I refer to as "Sovereign in Your Space" or assuming a leadership role in your personal journey. You possess authoritative control over both your energy field and consequently all five dimensions of your existence. Transformations may manifest abruptly and dramatically, although frequently they occur in a more gradual, understated manner, influencing one's emotions, actions, and overall demeanor in the realm of existence.

Putting Together Your Message

You assemble your information by formulating your message. Every presentation must be centeredaround a core message. During this stage, we will acquire the knowledge on crafting a persuasive message. The process of formulating your message is an indispensable and pivotal aspect in crafting an exceptional speech. The content conveyed represents the central focus of your presentation. It ought to meander through your presentation akin to interwoven strands in a textile. The main concept of your presentation revolves around the message. The communication is the essence of what you aim to convey to the intellect of your audience. It represents the cognitive impression derived from your presentation.

The process of crafting a concise message may appear to be a straightforward endeavor. However, this particular step tends to be significantly neglected within the entire speaking process, often regarded as a mere afterthought. The majority of individuals delivering presentations are predominantly focused on the process of preparing and presenting the content, often disregarding the crucial aspect of message formulation.

Goal-Driven Messages

Prior to creating the message, it is imperative that we gain a comprehensive understanding of the objective. Each presentation must have an objective. A goal can be defined as the intended course of action, representing the desired outcome that the audience is expected to undertake as a result of receiving the information. The initial action in formulating the message entails comprehending that the message is oriented towards achieving predefined objectives. The objective establishes the desired outcome you aim to achieve.

In order to define your objective, commence by envisioning the conclusion of your discourse. At the culmination of your presentation, it is anticipated that a response will be provided. The desired outcome is the objective you aim to accomplish. It is imperative that you have a well-defined understanding of the anticipated answer. It is imperative to comprehend the desired audience response. For all practical purposes, one would not embark upon a journey without having prior knowledge of the intended destination. In order to effectively deliver a presentation, one must possess a comprehensive understanding of their objective. The subsequent activity is designed to assist you in establishing your objective.

Would you like to persuade them to consider an alternative perspective? What is the novel concept or notion that you intend to instill within their consciousness?

Please feel free to allocate sufficient time for reflection before providing your responses. They embody a fundamental element in delineating your objective: the anticipated audience response.

Carefully examine the content you have composed. Please mark the responses that are of interest to you by underlining them. In the event that certain phrases exhibit similarity, it is advisable to amalgamate them. Examine and identify pivotal terms and expressions. Attempt to condense the objective into a singular statement that specifically centers around one or two primary concepts derived from the exercise. Your objective revolves around the accomplishment of that one statement.

Develop the Direct Mail Package

It is readily apparent to discern the majority of nonprofit correspondence...

Everything appears identical. If you assert my error, I will promptly direct you to inspect your correspondence in your mailbox. With few deviations from this norm, the vast majority of nonprofit correspondence is received in standard white, #10 window envelopes, featuring only a small emblem in the corner and an indicia that indicates the postal permit number of the mailing organization. Potentially, there could exist a line of text positioned above the window — functioning as a teaser — with the intention of providing you, the recipient, with a degree of understanding regarding the contents.

How frequently do you genuinely find yourself captivated by a correspondence you receive from a philanthropic institution? How often does your curiosity become stimulated? Alternatively, do you experience sentiments of indignation, sympathy, elation, empathy, etc.?

Similar to a skillfully crafted billboard, an effective package design is intended to capture your focus and distinguish itself amidst the assortment of mailings in your mailbox. Ultimately, well-crafted package designs ought to instill a sense of curiosity, leading one to eagerly unveil the contents contained within the envelope. And subsequently, sustain your inquisitiveness to effectively draw your attention towards the contents and constituents encompassed within said carrier envelope.

How is it that a meticulously crafted packaging is able to achieve these outcomes? Allow me to enumerate the various methods. A well-designed package...

1. Revitalizes and elevates the notion...

2. Penetrates the cognitive clutter to captivate the reader's focus and sustain her interest...

3. Demands readership right away...

4. Supports your corporate brand/identity/image...

5. Fosters a sense of connection with your cause/organization...

6. Facilitates and encourages a prompt and effortless response.

The Basic Package includes a carrier envelope, which serves as the outer envelope encompassing all other contents. Within this package, you will find the letter, a reply device commonly referred to as a turn-around document (TAD), and either a business reply envelope (BRE) or a courtesy reply envelope (RE). On occasion, the idea may necessitate supplementary materials, such as a pamphlet, a compact insert, or a "buck slip" (nicknamed for its approximate size of a dollar bill), intended to prompt a response through the provision of supplementary details, an exclusive offer, or a testimonial or other personalized message.

Effective package design takes into account the optimal utilization of these elements, aiming to create an appealing (or intentionally unappealing!) and aesthetically pleasing presentation that effectively captures the recipient's attention, while also being economical. The forthcoming chapter will provide a more comprehensive analysis of this subject matter.

A prosperous direct mail initiative necessitates meticulous strategizing and oversight, in addition to exemplary innovation. Occasionally, an individual may possess the capacity to oversee all elements of such a program; however, individuals with such comprehensive abilities are scarce and uncommon. Typically, the effective execution of the prescribed process necessitates the collaboration of multiple individuals who demonstrate exceptional proficiency in their respective roles: the manager/strategist, proficient copywriter and designer, as well as the diligent production coordinator responsible for consolidating the mailing list, coordinating the printing of materials, and ensuring the timely dispatch of the project.

Chapter 5:

Charismatically Cool

Possessing the knowledge of appropriate verbal expressions, effective communication techniques, and an astute sense of timing are indicative of a highly skilled individual in engaging conversations. However, there is an additional component that must be incorporated in order to attain proficiency in the art of casual conversation. What other observations can be made regarding accomplished individuals?

They're charismatic.

They appear to possess the capacity to captivate individuals during their conversations, particularly esteemed motivational speakers such as Tony Robbins and Les Brown. From the instant they commence speaking, they appear to captivate you. That's charisma at work. Certain individuals possess an inherent charm, whereas others must diligently cultivate their ability to attract others. It is frequently misconstrued as an innate aspect of an individual's character, yet it is actually an acquireable competence.

Similar to confidence, the development of charisma requires patience and dedication. With persistent effort and consistent practice, achieving charisma is ultimately within reach. Prior to undertaking the cultivation of your charismatic demeanor, it is imperative that you undertake the following steps:

Acquire Mastery in Fundamental Conversational Skills.

Prior to embarking on the cultivation of your charisma, it is imperative that you focus your efforts on fortifying the bedrock of your conversational aptitude, employing the methodologies elucidated in the preceding chapters. By closely observing individuals who possess charisma, one can discern their adeptness at engaging in conversation, initiating dialogue, sustaining its momentum, guiding its course, and capturing people's attention through their articulate expressions. They have attained proficient knowledge of the foundations.

It is imperative that you dedicate your efforts and engage in deliberate practice towards enhancing your aptitude for initiating casual conversations. Only once you have acquired sufficient self-assurance in those capabilities should you progress to the subsequent stage of charisma enhancement.

1. You are required to cultivate a cheerful countenance

And ensure that it is not contrived. The smile of an individual with charismatic qualities exudes a sense of calmness, authenticity, and approachability, yielding an atmosphere of warmth and friendliness. This is the smile that you should display while engaging in conversations with individuals. By adopting a smile, one can promptly create a sense of tranquility and ease for the other individual involved in the conversation. When one adopts a smiling countenance, their likeability is enhanced, and a sincere smile that emanates from one's face elicits a reciprocal smile from the other person. Possessing a genuine smile is a fundamental attribute necessary for individuals striving to exude charisma. Engage in the daily activity of practicing a self-directed smile before a reflective surface, ensuring a state of relaxation and contentment while doing so, and carefully observe the resulting outcome. Does it appear sufficiently authentic?" or "Does it give off a sense of naturalness? Does it appear rigid or contrived in any manner? To effectively convey an authentic smile during a casual conversation, it is imperative to possess a genuine desire to actively interact with the individual. When one desires to engage in an activity, it no longer imparts a sense of compulsion or obligation.

2. Exhibit an Appropriate Level of Eye Contact

It is essential to maintain eye contact during a conversation, while ensuring that you do not engage in a prolonged, intense gaze that could potentially come across as confrontational or threatening.

Maintaining direct visual engagement during a conversation is of utmost importance as it conveys to the interlocutor that they are deserving of your undivided attention, revealing a strong concentration and sincere interest in their discourse. Have you ever encountered a situation in which the individual seemed preoccupied or displayed a lack of sustained focus on you while engaged in conversation? It can be extremely vexing and bordering on discourteous! The most appropriate duration for maintaining eye contact is to sustain a person's gaze for one second beyond what is typically observed. In the context of small talk practice sessions, it is advisable to cultivate the habitual practice of maintaining consistent eye contact. This can be achieved by prolonging one's gaze slightly, and only momentarily diverting it elsewhere without fully averting one's head during the process of blinking. Engage in this activity in front of a mirror, rehearse it during morning encounters with individuals, among your colleagues at your place of employment, and while engaging with the cashier who is facilitating your grocery transactions. There exist numerous opportunities for you to engage in practice; it is merely a matter of initiating your utilization of them until mastery is attained.

Chapter II - Engaging in Art-Related Conversations

When considering small talk, it is possible that we associate it with an apathetic response to individuals with whom we have little desire to engage in conversation, or hearing discussions that hold minimal significance to us. To this day, the act of engaging in trivial conversation indeed fulfills significant objectives in fostering relationships, cultivating one's personality, enhancing knowledge, and developing skills. Casual conversation pertains to the practice of initiating dialogue with individuals to whom one has limited familiarity and may not necessarily seek to establish a deeper relationship. Engaging in casual conversation tends to make numerous individuals feel uneasy and awkward. Thus far, a deficiency in the skill of engaging in casual conversation, especially with unfamiliar individuals, may adversely impact our aptitude to effectively interact in professional settings, communities, and with the general public.

Hence, when faced with the uncomfortable state of isolation amidst others while passing time in situations that necessitate waiting, the ensuing discussion outlines several advantages of engaging in small talk, which will undoubtedly alleviate the tension.

Creates Network

Engaging in casual conversations with unfamiliar individuals can foster connections that, under fortunate circumstances, can evolve into prospects for new employment or a career path.

Moreover, such interactions may lead us to chance encounters with outstanding services we have long sought or enable us to establish relationships with a group of individuals whom we deeply admire. Engaging in casual conversation can lead us to valuable networking opportunities. When individuals with whom you engage in casual conversation choose to share your name with others, it is probable that they will also disseminate pertinent details regarding your expertise and background. Casual conversation is a potent tool wielded by individuals engaged in the field of networking business.

As an illustration, I possess an extensive understanding of computer hardware, making me well-versed in technical matters. This proficiency enables me to offer freelance hardware servicing as a means of generating income. Those who have knowledge of this matter include my intimate acquaintances, colleagues, relatives, and select individuals to whom I have provided my assistance. Through engaging in casual conversation, individuals may mention your name to others, ultimately expanding your professional network and leading to an increased number of business transactions, consequently augmenting your profitability.

Make you Smarter

Engaging in casual conversation holds significance as it enhances one's intellectual capabilities. Indeed, engaging in conversation fosters intellectual enhancement as it facilitates the exchange of ideas and knowledge between oneself and the interlocutor, thereby yielding increased cognitive benefits, particularly when the topic being discussed is of personal interest. According to a study conducted by researchers at the University of Michigan, it has been determined that engaging in peaceful social interactions has the ability to enhance our problem-solving capabilities. According to Oscar

Ybarra, the psychologist who conducted the study, certain social interactions prompt individuals to engage in mind-reading and adopt alternative perspectives. This phenomenon was evident in a specific instance during a casual conversation with a taxi driver while I was travelling, as I pondered the rapid decline in crude oil prices. In a polite and deferential manner, I inquired, "Sir, would you happen to possess any knowledge pertaining to the factors causing the significant drop in crude oil prices since the fourth quarter of 2014?" In response to this straightforward query, the driver offered a concise explanation, stating, "The drop is attributed to the surplus supply from OPEC, particularly Saudi Arabia, coupled with reduced demand." As the United States represents a significant consumer, it has decided to enhance the production capacity of domestic crude oil drilling companies. The OPEC-Saudi Arabia oil product witnessed a decline due to the manipulation of crude oil prices resulting from a sudden surge in demand for crude oil in China, which was facilitated by China's assistance. I acquired insights into the current state of the global crude oil market. If I encounter a similar inquiry in the future, I would be able to provide the correct response to the inquirer.

Provide your thoughts or observations regarding a widely circulated video.

Viral recordings possess significant communicative influence. Numerous individuals engage in viewing recordings during their leisure hours or receive information about them through acquaintances or colleagues. If you opt to employ this system, please ensure that the video you view adheres to appropriate workplace standards. Please be presented with an example: Have you had the opportunity to view the footage portraying a child dozing off in the container of frozen yogurt? Ideally, this will instigate a discourse on other captivating recordings or topics of mainstream culture.

Be direct

In certain instances, initiating a conversation by directly expressing your intentions or desires can often be considered the most effective approach. For example, if you happen to be misplaced, kindly ask for directions. To partake in a midday meal with an individual, make it evident. Allow me to present an alternative suggestion: On this inaugural day, my understanding of the precise location to dine remains elusive. Do you anticipate any potential issues in the event that I were to join you?

Request help

Seeking assistance is an effective approach to initiating a conversation. Depending on the situation at hand, it may be necessary for you to seek assistance from a specific individual rather than anyone in close proximity.

Consider this framework: As I have not previously operated from this office, I am unfamiliar with the operational procedures it follows. Do you anticipate any issues with assisting me?

Analyze typical areas of interest

In specific instances, it is evident that you possess a mutual interest with an individual who is not a part of the group. Please employ the sign that you perceive as an initial point for the conversation. For example: I notice that you also support our local basketball team. I had the opportunity to attend a game a week ago. How about yourself? Gaining knowledge about your new associate and exchanging information about oneself generally leads to the discovery of shared interests. Focus on these topics and discuss them in detail; the discovery of new information remains unpredictable. Nevertheless, you may find someone else to engage in this hobby with. If no common interests are found, then it is advised to simply remain at ease. Not every individual you encounter is destined to become your closest companion. Congratulations on having made it this far in our discussion!

Present an insightful observation

Inaugurating a conversation with a stranger can be further enhanced by making an observation about the surrounding environment or situation.

situation in which you find yourself. This methodology is most effective when there is a specific aspect worth highlighting, such as: I've noticed your preference for using the handset instead of a headset. This type of comment allows the external party to express their own perspectives on the matter.

Observe a shared characteristic

When you are certain that both parties involved share a shared quality, employ this procedure. Engaging in a conversation about a shared attribute is often an excellent means of forging an immediate connection. Consider

Regarding this particular model, I happened to notice that you provided your endorsement using your left hand. Coincidentally, I am also left-handed. When intriguing attributes are at play, a significant number of individuals engage in discourse regarding the affiliation.

Kindly inquire about their relevant experience

Obtaining relevant details regarding their background is a proficient and hospitable approach to initiate a conversation. Consider this illustration: Welcome to our collective! May I inquire as to your previous whereabouts prior to joining us at this juncture?

6. Stay updated on current events.

Contemporary affairs provide an excellent gateway for commencement. In the event that you and the unfamiliar individual hold contrasting perspectives, it is most advisable to engage in discussions centeredaround non-political occurrences. Consider inquiring about a nearby celebration or a recent literary or cinematic masterpiece that has recently hit the market.

7. Offer to assist

Extending assistance to an unfamiliar individual encountering difficulties with a task serves as an excellent means to commence a dialogue. Given the location and context of the interaction, one possible illustration could be employed, such as the following:

Please take into account the following situation: "May I assist you in transporting that box? Are you unfamiliar with the building?"

8. Share a fascinating fact.

This approach is most effective when you find yourself in an environment or circumstances where your captivating detail is germane. When employed appropriately, this methodology can serve as an excellent means of initiating a dialogue with an unfamiliar individual.

9. Seek their feedback.

To initiate a dialogue, inquire about the viewpoint of an unfamiliar individual. If you happen to be on your lunch break or in search of writing instruments in your office's supply cabinet, this strategy is quite commendable.

10. Seek lunch recommendations.

Initiating a conversation with an individual by seeking information concerning their preferred lunch establishment is an effective approach. Due to its expedient nature, this proves to be particularly advantageous when one finds themselves in an elevator or awaiting transportation services such as a taxi or public transit.

11. Provide feedback on a widely-viewed video by leaving a comment.

Viral videos can serve as an effective vehicle for initiating a discourse. During their leisure hours, numerous individuals engage in the consumption of videos either by actively seeking them or through referrals from acquaintances or colleagues.

It is anticipated that this may engender a discourse pertaining to additional captivating videos or subjects within popular culture.

Meetups

For certain individuals, adhering to the framework of a prearranged occasion is considerably more effortless. All arrangements are made by another individual, allowing you the opportunity to effortlessly engage with others and enjoy yourself.

This alleviates the burden and facilitates a more relaxed and uninhibited environment, allowing individuals to engage in social interactions with diminished focus on the specific occasion at hand. Furthermore, the act of attending these events facilitates the development of shared interests, leading to natural conversation starters.

Cultural Events

Participating in an occasion that holds cultural significance for you presents an avenue to engage with women who share a similar heritage or, at the very least, a shared enthusiasm. Festivals, fairs, and parades provide conducive environments for initiating conversations based on shared interests.

Cultural and Scholarly Occasions

Cultural institutions such as museums, art galleries, literary readings, and author signings provide excellent opportunities to socialize and meet women. It is imperative to possess a certain level of familiarity pertaining to the purpose of your presence. Do not commit the error of squandering an opportunity by hastily imparting information pertaining to an incorrect artist.

What Are the Signs?

So, how can one ascertain if she is receptive to engaging in conversation and playful interaction?

Primarily, seek out indications of non-verbal communication. We shall persistently address the matter of body language, pertaining to both the female individual and yourself, as it constitutes a paramount aspect of effective communication with women.

Is she exhibiting signs of being reserved? Is she smiling? Does she appear to be prepared to engage in violent behavior towards someone?

Is she maintaining visual contact with you? If she averts her gaze after briefly making eye contact with you without returning it, it is likely an indication that she is not interested in you as a potential partner.

However, were you able to observe her discreetly expressing interest in you? That is an unmistakable indication! Should she gaze at you from head to toe, accompanied by a subtle smile, you have indeed caught her discreetly appraising you. Make an effort to establish eye contact with her and reciprocate with a friendly smile. After completing the task, proceed to the designated location and initiate an interaction to greet others. It presents a remarkable chance to playfully tease her or jest about apprehending her gaze.

The Self Touch

Research has substantiated the psychological phenomenon wherein women, when exhibiting an attraction towards men, display a tendency to engage in tactile contact with specific regions of their body. Certain women engage in hair manipulation or fiddle with their hair, while others may opt to touch their neck. It is within your discretion to determine whether you are the cause of the reaction or if the scratching merely coincided with a momentary itch. Combine the physical contact with direct eye contact, and the indications appear favorable.

You frequently encounter her.

Should a woman express interest, she may furnish you with opportunities. Do you believe that it is merely coincidental that you consistently encounter her amidst the gathering or occasion? There is a possibility that she has been observing you with the intention of engaging in flirtatious conversation at a suitable moment. Seize the opportunity! Furthermore, engage in playful social interaction and incorporate it into conversation. Attempt to inquire if she has been monitoring your actions.

Similarly, a collision or incidental contact with you. Yes, it is possible that such incidents might occur unintentionally. However, based on my personal experience, I would like to impart an important lesson to all:

women are not devoid of intelligence. They possess a precise understanding of game strategies and provide you with precisely the amount of information required for you to seize the opportunity. This scenario could potentially serve as an assessment, in which she is observing and evaluating the extent of your masculinity. Will you talk to her?

Numerous individuals share the same apprehension towards communication as you do.

There are others who share your apprehension towards communication. The issue of communication anxiety is a prevalent challenge encountered by numerous individuals. Parents struggle with their children, couples struggle with each other, employees struggle with co-workers, and so on.

The apprehension towards communication is a prevalent sentiment among nearly all individuals. Your communication difficulties do not indicate any deficiency on your part; however, it is incumbent upon you to address and resolve them. If you failed to resolve those issues, you would encounter significant challenges in your life.

Regardless, recognizing that you are not the only one in your struggle can prove to be beneficial. You are not the sole individual endeavoring to conquer your uncertainties.

Apprehensions impede our capacity to establish acquaintances, foster connections, make progress in our professional endeavors, and attain economic security. Despite the capability of the internet and social media to enable us to engage with countless individuals, sometimes even without the need for verbal communication, it may not be a prudent approach to effectively attain our objectives. This holds particular significance when attempting to mitigate the unease associated with interpersonal communication.

So, what are the prevailing concerns regarding communication among individuals? Undoubtedly, public speaking emerges as the most prevalent form of social phobia. Indeed, there's no denying the fact that the prospect of being center stage, with countless eyes meticulously observing our every move and gesture, can be quite daunting.

Encountering unfamiliar individuals presents itself as a prominent source of social unease. If one possesses a reserved disposition, it is likely that they are acquainted with the uncomfortable sensation experienced when in an unfamiliar setting, encompassed by enigmatic countenances. Additional social anxieties encompass soliciting aid, inviting someone on a date, engaging in sales endeavors, petitioning for career advancement, broaching sensitive subjects, receiving affirming evaluations, and the like.

We have all experienced such occasions when we are immersed in the bliss of a splendid day, only for our emotional state to abruptly shift. Why is that? What happened? What was the cause behind the sudden transition from a state of positive emotion to that of negative sentiment? Is there any course of action that I may undertake?

These are merely a handful of the multitude of thoughts that emerge when we observe a shift in our environment, a shift in our emotional state prompted by our significant other, or a shift in the emotional state of our significant other.

Accompanied by these inquiries shall arise the ambiguity and apprehension of grappling with such a circumstance. Subsequently, the fundamental inquiry arises: "What measures must be undertaken to mitigate the apprehension?"

In numerous marital relationships, a prevalent tendency towards conversational apprehension can be observed. When an event occurs, individuals tend to engage in a mental dialogue, oftentimes centeringaround a multitude of inquiries. In many cases, it appears that individuals frequently embrace a cautious approach, commonly referred to as the \"play it safe\" mindset. There are various reasons why individuals may choose not to address this latest issue. These rationales include: dealing with concurrent stressful matters and wanting to avoid adding to their already significant list of concerns; experiencing a positive period and desiring to maintain this momentum; attempting to prevent the escalation of an argument; being mindful of others' emotions and not wanting to cause harm; growing weary of receiving criticism or self-doubt that talking about the matter will yield any positive results. Regardless of the specific excuse, we tend to neglect these thoughts on a daily basis, but at what expense?

Permitting the escalation of these issues may result in various detrimental consequences for a relationship. Unbeknownst to them, a gradual accumulation of anger takes place, leading to the introduction of suspicion into their relationship. Concomitantly, negative emotions intensify, resulting in heightened irritability and discontent, creating an environment where partners are prone to growing apart. Frequently, it is observed that one of the individuals involved in the relationship remains completely unaware of the gradual formation of an emotional void, firmly believing in their ability to shoulder the entirety of the emotional burden independently. As a result, there is a gradual accumulation of resentment towards the partner due to their perceived lack of concern, assistance, or recollection. In the interim, the other individual remains ensnared as they have been thoroughly caught off guard by this disclosure.

Managing your emotional intelligence can be effectively accomplished if one possesses the requisite knowledge and skills to do so. There are numerous endeavors you can undertake to enhance your overall intellectual capacity.

Strategies for enhancing your emotional intelligence

There exist three pivotal actions one can undertake in order to enhance their emotional intelligence:

Mitigate the potential hazards presented by stress." "Prevent stress from becoming a source of danger." "Ensure that stress does not pose a significant risk." "Minimize the adverse impact of stress.

Initially, it is imperative to mitigate the strains or pressures that you are currently experiencing in your daily existence. It is imperative to commence by actively recognizing instances of stress. Consider instances where your musculature remains taut or your respiratory capacity appears diminished.

You must subsequently acquire the skills to effectively cope with stress. Take a step back for a moment and see how the stress will move through or fade over time, for instance.

Exercise caution and attentiveness to your environment.

The crux of developing emotional intelligence lies in cultivating a comprehensive comprehension of one's surroundings and their underlying dynamics. Engage in detailed observation of your immediate environment, by attentively noting the events transpiring, the actions undertaken by individuals, and similar factors.

Conduct a diligent examination of how individuals are reacting to specific stimuli. Observe the manner in which these individuals are engaging in conversation with you and how they are reacting to your actions. Perhaps it would be possible to discreetly observe an individual in order to gauge their behavior.

One must consider the appropriate emotions to employ in a given situation. It is imperative not to harbor the assumption that one possesses limitless capabilities upon entering a room, as it is conceivable that certain individuals may feel uneasy or lack assurance regarding the circumstances at hand.

Look at nonverbal communication.

The significance of nonverbal communication may surpass your initial perception. One must meticulously observe individuals' conduct within specific circumstances.

Direct your attention towards observing others to gain an understanding of their current situation. Consider how a discourse may involve aspects such as modifications in an individual's behavior. If an individual maintains a close proximity of their body while speaking, it is indicative of a reluctance to engage in conversation or exchange ideas with you.

In certain scenarios, it is plausible that an individual's vocal inflection or countenance may undergo alteration. This can lead to the perception that an individual may be concealing certain convictions or concepts during communication.

Please ensure that you maintain eye contact with individuals you engage in conversation or interact with. Making direct eye contact can assist in discerning whether an individual is displaying interest in your presence or exhibiting a positive response to a given situation. If an individual's gaze does not exhibit complete concentration on one's self, it implies that the person is experiencing excessive stress or preoccupation with other thoughts. In the interim, an individual's reaction can be assessed by observing the potential ocular manifestations during their response. There is a possibility that an individual may respond by diverting their gaze or displaying restrained behavior when engaging with others.

7. Language barriers

Currently, numerous corporations operate across various nations. In the majority of such organizations, the communication across different geographical locations occurs using the English language. However, it should be noted that each individual possesses their own unique accent and is likewise subject to the impact of cultural influences and mannerisms. The presence of these linguistic barriers further compounds the difficulty of communication. Several recommendations can facilitate more efficient and fruitful communication amidst the challenge of language barriers.

Utter words with measured pace – One fundamental assistance the speaker can offer is to enunciate words slowly and articulately. Whilst the language of communication could possibly be your mother tongue, it may not necessarily hold true for your audience. Demonstrate reverence by adopting a deliberate and articulate demeanor.

Engage everyone – Exert a concerted effort to engage all your audience members in the dissemination of information. Make an effort to gather targeted feedback from a wide range of individuals, in order to validate the comprehension of the matter at hand. This serves to confirm to the audience that their significance is recognized, and presents them with a chance to seek further information or address any uncertainties they may have.

Cultural disparities - Endeavor to comprehend the cultural nuances and etiquettes of your audience. There exist numerous methods to accomplish this task. Acquire a comprehensive understanding of their culture by engaging in activities such as reading literature focused on their customs, conducting thorough research using online resources, embarking on visits to their nation, observing their behaviorsfirsthand, watching sports events broadcasted from their country, staying informed through their news outlets, immersing oneself in their cinematic productions, or accessing translated versions of their literary works. This will provide you with insight into their culture - The work environment in Japan differs from that in the United States, as it is characterized by distinct perspectives on work, varied social structures, and differing values relating to family. Divergent perspectives on acceptable communication may exist between various communities, as what is deemed appropriate within one group might be perceived as inappropriate and disparaging in another.

Conduct direct interactions – Despite incurring expenses, it is advisable to promote team leaders to engage in personal meetings with their teams, spanning different nations, at regular intervals. Even periodic annual visits, or gatherings can be effective. Engaging in personal encounters allows individuals to gain a deeper comprehension of one another.

8. A Parting Joke

Allow us to conclude with a brief jest:

The politician's address is laced with an abundance of tedium. Suddenly, an individual materializes before the lectern, brandishing a substantial implement. He commences to traverse in front of the podium.

The statesman becomes anxious and conveys the information to the gentleman. Would you prefer me to conclude my speech, Sir, if it is not to your liking?

The gentleman retorts, "Oh, no, sir. Please, I implore you to proceed." I am currently endeavoring to locate the individual responsible for extending an invitation for your presence here today."

Virtual/Remote Meetings *

14. It is advisable to prompt all participants to provide an introduction (or verbally acknowledge their presence) at the commencement of the meeting, as well as identifying themselves each time they contribute to the discussion (except in the case of video/web conferencing or long-established teams where individuals are widely recognized).

15. Institute clear guidelines regarding the engagement of all participants,

including periodic pauses for summarization, solicitation of questions, fostering discussions, and seeking clarification.

16. Please guarantee the timely or advanced distribution of visual or graphic materials to all individuals, using methods such as email, download, network access, shared document sites, and so on.

17. Kindly advise all individuals to articulate their speech at a moderate pace, enunciate with precision, and direct their voices towards microphones, speakerphones, or remote phones. Additionally, please emphasize the importance of requesting a repetition in the event that any communication is not clearly audible.

18. Recommend that individuals who are participating remotely be encouraged to utilize headsets and activate the "Mute" function on their phones in order to minimize any potential disturbance caused by

background noise during a virtual meeting.

19. Keep to the schedule.

20. Promptly disseminate a comprehensive summary of the meeting, including pertinent information regarding resolutions and subsequent tasks.

21. Arrange any necessary subsequent meetings.

22. Please execute any action items that were decided upon during the meeting.

When Conducted In Person

23. Condense the duration of your meetings! It has been reported by a majority of managers that

approximately 50% of meeting time is squandered.

24. Each meeting must be accompanied by a publicly accessible agenda that addresses the fundamental question: What is the purpose of investing time in this meeting? What is the duration of its longevity? Who's attending? What are the expectations?

25. Commence and conclude punctually. Convening gatherings constitutes a major expenditure that does not have a direct impact on the financial statements. Determine the solution - a four-hour meeting involving four employees earning an annual salary of $50,000 each results in a total expenditure of $400 in terms of employee time. Please acknowledge the significance of the investment involved in this meeting.

26. Morning meetings held in the early hours of the day are generally regarded as optimal. Individuals exhibit a heightened sense of vitality, as they are less fatigued. The prospective obstacles of the day remain dormant, thereby increasing the likelihood of punctuality for all.

27. Initiate your meetings by commencing with the utmost significant agenda item.

28. Enforce predefined time constraints on individuals' ability to present their arguments. An activity that significantly consumes time is engaging in futile conflicts. Implement time restrictions for each item and proceed accordingly.

29. Conclude the meeting by summarizing the assigned duties, scheduled timeframe for completion,

and the means of communication to ensure clarity among all participants.

How to Enhance Self-Confidence

Do you comprehend the extent to which a lack of confidence can negatively impact your well-being? Confidence is crucial, particularly when eliciting a favorable impression during an informal conversation. Having a sense of confidence empowers individuals with the certainty that they are capable of handling their current circumstances adeptly, thus exerting influence over the trajectory of a conversation.

1. Mind Over Matter

Self-assurance originates within one's psyche, and it is a mental state that rests solely within an individual's ability to modify. One must have a desire to alter their perception of oneself and release any unfavorable associations they may possess. There exist numerous approaches through which you can enhance and fortify your mindset gradually. Assure yourself that you possess an inherent sense of self-assurance, demonstrating tremendous capability to effectively manage any obstacle encountered. An example of accomplishing this objective is through the practice of meditation, which serves as a beneficial exercise for the overall well-being of the mind, body, and spirit. An alternative approach involves employing affirmations or transcribing them onto small adhesive notes, strategically placing them in prominent locations within your environment. By consistently immersing yourself in these positive affirmations, you create a continuous reminder of encouragement. Once again, the focus lies in discovering the approach that suits you most effectively; yet it is advisable to commence the process of fortifying your mindset towards cultivating a more positive outlook.

2. Determine Areas Requiring Improvement

Self-doubt poses a formidable mental barrier that must be surmounted in order to cultivate self-assurance and recognize one's true potential. You have been burdened with lingering self-doubt over an extended period, rendering it seemingly inconceivable to adopt an alternative mindset. It may pose a challenge initially, nevertheless, it is imperative to embark on this journey if one aspires to initiate their personal growth and evolution into a superior rendition of themselves. Commence by compiling a catalogue of what you perceive to be the domains necessitating improvement. After concluding the task, proceed to compile a comprehensive catalogue of potential recommendations pertaining to the enhancement of said areas. It is not imperative for the modifications to be large-scale and immediate in nature. It will not be advantageous for you if you are experiencing a sense of being overwhelmed. Commence with modest objectives that are within your reach, and proceed to iterate this process as you progressively accomplish them.

3. Recognize your accomplishments

Have you managed a specific task exceptionally effectively today? Did the outcome exceed your initial expectations? It is imperative that we commence recognizing it. It is strongly recommended that you develop a practice, henceforth, of acknowledging and commending yourself for your achievements on a consistent basis. In the end, it is considered a noteworthy accomplishment, thus deserving acknowledgment. As an illustration, should you have had a notably prosperous exchange of pleasantries during the course of the day, commendable accomplishment! Admirable performance. Indulge yourself in something delightful as a token of appreciation. You ought to take pride in your achievements, as they contribute to the gradual development of your self-assurance.

4. Compile an inventory of your strengths

At times, it is more convenient to embrace a belief when it is presented in written form before one's eyes. If you encounter difficulty in compiling a roster of your advantageous attributes, you may seek the assistance of your familial and social circle to accomplish this task. Kindly request them to share their perspectives on what aspects they find most admirable about you and your areas of expertise or strengths. Request their assistance in determining and discerning your individual strengths. Furthermore, by considering the perspectives of others, particularly those that may have previously eluded your attention, you can enhance your self-assurance as well. After you have assembled your list, make it a regular practice to review it daily until you have a strong conviction in every aspect recorded and notice a discernible boost in your level of self-assurance.

5. It is essential to have a pleasing appearance in order to experience a positive sense of well-being.

Your self-perception significantly influences the level of confidence you possess. To what extent do you allocate time towards tending to your appearance and the manner in which you project yourself? Is your hair meticulously groomed? Do you tend to don properly fitting attire? Your initial appearance will be the foremost aspect that individuals will perceive when you introduce yourself, and dedicating time to enhance your appearance and confidence will prove beneficial. There is no necessity to purchase a new wardrobe in order to appear suitable; rather, it is advisable to make use of your existing clothing. Ensure that your garments consistently maintain a clean appearance, offer utmost comfort, and instill a sense of personal well-being. The heightened sense of self-esteem directly correlates to an increased level of confidence one exudes.

The Initial Phase: Managing and Addressing Emotions of Anger

The initial stage in addressing anger entails effectively managing and addressing one's anger. When experiencing a sense of inner turmoil, it is probable that you will respond in an aggressive manner to circumstances that evoke discomfort. Presented herein are several recommendations that will assist you in effectively managing your feelings of anger:

Do not allow resentment to cultivate: If there is a persistent issue that is causing distress, it is essential to address it promptly. Acknowledge the reality that you are experiencing anger regarding a certain matter, in order to address it in an efficient manner. During moments of introspection, it is imperative to pose inquiries such as "Is my anger justifiable?" and "What is the root cause of my anger?" By delving into these minor concerns, one will discern that they are indeed trivial issues that are causing distress and impeding effective communication.

Communicate with Others: In the event that you perceive that your anger stems from someone else's actions, adopt a receptive stance and engage in dialogue with the individual in question. Employ affirmative statements to effectively convey your argument.

Establish Objectives: It is imperative to ascertain your desired outcomes resulting from a shift in your character. You should exercise prudence in considering the potential impact of your actions on future circumstances.

Seek Resolutions: Once you have discerned the source of your anger, endeavor to discover viable remedies that will preclude the reoccurrence of this matter in the foreseeable future.

Managing the Escalation of Anger from Others

Recognize the individual's frustration: Convey to them that you understand their anger, while expressing your commitment to resolving the issue.

Commence the Journey: Following the identification of the issue, the logical progression entails seeking out a resolution. Be the pioneer in discovering the solution. Propose to the individual your earnest intention to address the issue through a mutual discussion in a seated and proactive manner.

Maintain composure: When confronted with anger, ensure that your demeanor remains non-threatening to the individual involved. In the event that you are not composed, there is a high probability that you will incite the hostility of the other individual. Maintain a composed posture throughout the duration of the conversation. Ensure that your vocal modulation remains consistent and subdued. It is essential to adopt an assertive approach while avoiding passivity or aggression.

Pay attention: By acquiring the ability to actively listen to an individual's perspective, you have already achieved a significant portion of your objective. Attempt to convey to the individual the comprehension you have attained through the act of attentive listening. Once you have received verification of your comprehension of the situation, handle it in a suitable manner.

Practice acceptance: Engaging in confrontations often undermines our ability to acknowledge the validity of certain viewpoints. Do not entirely disregard the other person's opinion. If you acknowledge that the anger expressed by the other individual is justified, confess your agreement.

Apologize: Should you be aware of your culpability, acknowledge it. Offer an apology in instances where you have made a mistake. It is more advantageous than engaging in incessant self-defense.

Comprehend the sentiment of frustration: It is essential to acknowledge the reality that anger is an inherent emotion experienced by all individuals, including oneself. It is advisable not to dismiss or disregard the anger of the other individual. The objective is to manage the other individual's anger in the most constructive manner feasible. This is the cornerstone to fostering a relationship that is characterized by optimal well-being and the absence of negativity.

It alleviates a significant amount of anxiety.

Life presents numerous challenges and concerns. It is not surprising that approximately 40 million Americans are affected by anxiety, as reported by Harvard Health (n.d.). This can instill a sense of fear or apprehension towards taking risks, consequently causing one to restrain oneself. Fundamentally, anxiety serves as an impediment to fulfilling one's full potential.

Once you attain a more profound comprehension of your life's purpose, circumstances will undergo a positive transformation. You will experience a reduction in anxiety as you gain a heightened sense of lucidity regarding the direction in which you are progressing. As you embark on the pursuit of your life's purpose, a sense of anticipation will supplant any feelings of apprehension. Your primary emphasis should be on the attainment of your aspirations rather than dwelling on the pessimistic ruminations that accompany anxiety.

It is evident that a decrease in anxiety leads to an increase in well-being. You will experience a heightened sense of serenity in relation to the choices you make and exhibit steadfast assurance towards the path that lies ahead. This enables a more streamlined approach to assertiveness by directing your attention solely to matters of genuine significance, rather than wasting time on trivialities.

Life is inherently unpredictable, but maintaining a focus on the broader perspective enables us to confront unforeseen circumstances with resilience and determination.

Alright, having discussed the reasons behind seeking purpose, I understand that some of you may be wondering about the practical steps to take. Rest assured, I believe I can provide you with a suitable response.

Methods for Determining Personal Desires

In a world replete with multifarious prospects, it is not uncommon for us to be confronted with a dilemma of uncertainty regarding our desires. For each available choice, there exist twice as many alternative options to select from. First and foremost, I am confronted with the question of where to begin.

In my opinion, the crucial inquiry lies not in the matter of 'where' but rather in the aspect of 'when.' The prospect of awakening at the age of 60, burdened with profound discontent as a result of belatedly recognizing a life lived out of accordance with personal desires, is truly disheartening. What an unfortunate squandering it would be! Hence, the unequivocal response to our initial inquiry of 'When should we commence?' is emphatically at this very moment.

Once you have obtained clarity about your aspirations in life, you have progressed closer towards transforming them into tangible achievements. Considering the circumstances, it is unrealistic to anticipate the accomplishment of a goal without possessing a clear understanding of its nature.

To commence the pursuit of discovering your purpose, consider the following methodology:

Envision the Undesirable Outcomes

Humans are strange. We encounter difficulty in precisely identifying our preferences, yet require only a moment to discern our dislikes. But it makes sense. Why would we not exhibit efficiency in recognizing unfavorable circumstances that we desire to evade? We are cognizant of our aversion towards poverty, illness, and suffering, among other undesirable circumstances.

Fortunately, your skill in discerning your dislikes greatly facilitates the process of recognizing your preferences. A prevalent disparity often exists between two cognitive states. In this instance, there exists a contrast between an unfavorable outcome and a favorable outcome. You may utilize one as a point of reference for the other. Take happiness, for example. We would lack the understanding of the experience if we were devoid of sadness as a point of reference.

If you encounter difficulty in determining your desires, perhaps directing your attention towards what you do not desire is an approach worth considering. After compiling the list of undesirable elements, one can proceed to reverse the perspective and record the corresponding contrasting conditions.

Strategies For Cultivating Assertiveness On An Individual Level

Acquiring the ability to make assertive statements is a trainable aptitude, thus there is no need for concern if one lacks it at present. I likely resembled you—a individual whose manner of communication tended to be passive rather than assertive. During the course of a conversation, it is possible that an individual within the group may interrupt me, prompting a thought along the lines of "Alright, this interruption is of no significant consequence." I had an inclination to avoid causing any inconvenience, and to be frank, I was experiencing apprehension. I was uncertain about how to commence my journey, as I harbored doubts regarding the prospect of attaining increased confidence and efficacy in articulating my perspectives.

When recounting this narrative, individuals anticipate the presence of a pivotal moment, an occurrence that would undoubtedly enhance the story's liveliness. However, including such an element would compromise its veracity. Indeed, the veracity of the matter is that I simply desired a transition. I aspired to enhance my capabilities, achieve higher levels of success, and establish myself as a role model for others. I aspired to acquire the ability to assert myself, ensuring that my perspective would be duly considered and not dismissed arbitrarily.

I would like to present the following guidelines that proved instrumental in facilitating improved and more efficient means of communication during my personal journey:

Assess your manner of communication.

In my unwavering conviction, I firmly advocate for the primacy of personal responsibility, urging individuals to embark upon introspection and self-improvement. Thus, the opening chapter meticulously delves into the diverse communication styles. Have you already determined your own?

Do you refrain from speaking when the situation warrants it? Do you affirmatively accept supplementary tasks despite being unable to accommodate further assignments? It appears that you have a preference for a passive communication style.

Do you have a tendency to make hasty judgments or assign blame? Is there an inclination among individuals to experience apprehension or anxiety in conversing with you? Should this be the case, it is possible that you exhibit an assertive mode of communication.

If you remain uncertain, it would be advisable to inquire with your acquaintances and relatives. When I inquired, they promptly informed me of the particular communication style that I possess. Furthermore, I have discovered that a highly effective method for gauging one's communication style is to carefully observe and keep records of their behavioral patterns.

For instance, on the following day, you may record the occasion when there was an opportunity to express yourself but you refrained from doing so, thereby exemplifying a passive communication approach. In a different manner, you might consider acknowledging the fact that you exhibited an exaggerated response upon receiving an unfavorable remark from your friend regarding your recently acquired apparel. Now you are aware that you are inclined towards an assertive approach. Prior to initiating any adjustments, it is imperative to have a clear comprehension of your own communication style.

Personalize your statements

Utilizing "I" statements enables individuals to express their thoughts or emotions while maintaining a non-confrontational or intimidating tone. For example, opt for the phrase "I hold a different perspective" in lieu of "You are incorrect." In case you have a favor to ask, employ the phrase "I kindly request your assistance with this matter" instead of "You must do this." By doing so, you redirect the attention from their actions towards expressing your sentiments regarding the situation.

Using "I" statements serves to mitigate the impact of your statement and diminish the force of your allegations when shifting the focus from others to yourself. This creates the perception that you are not passing judgment, but merely articulating the impact of their actions on your person. To put it succinctly, commencing a sentence with "You..." tends to convey a sense of judgment or criticism, potentially causing others to adopt a defensive stance. Beginning the sentence with the pronoun "I" places greater emphasis on one's own emotions and the impact of the other person's behavior. Furthermore, it demonstrates a higher level of personal responsibility for one's reactions and a decreased inclination to assign blame. This approach aids in mitigating defensiveness in the individual, exemplifies the act of assuming accountability, and propels both parties towards fostering constructive transformation. For example:

It is imperative that you cease such actions immediately.

I kindly request that you cease such behavior.

When applied to factual statements rather than judgments or labels, this framework offers a direct and non-confrontational approach, fostering a greater sense of accountability, to communicate the impact of one's behavior on others. This approach serves as an effective means of presenting your standpoint, for it is inherently challenging to contest. What grounds do skeptics possess to assert its inaccuracy? This concerns your emotional state. You are unable to cease experiencing the emotions you have simply because others perceive them as incorrect.

Commence the conduct initially, subsequently delineate the outcomes, and finally articulate the sentiments. The formula is as follows:

Upon observing your behavior, I have noticed that it leads to undesirable consequences, thereby evoking certain emotions within me.

Examples:

Upon your tardy arrival, I am compelled to patiently wait, thereby evoking feelings of frustration within me.

When you inform the children regarding the permissibility of an action that I have explicitly prohibited, it erodes a portion of my parental authority, and I perceive it as undermining.

When you raise your voice, I perceive it as a form of aggression.

Ensure that your expressions are both concise and precise. Maintain vigilance over your conduct throughout the course of a day and endeavor to integrate diverse structures as exemplified previously.

Chapter III: Elevating Your Listening Proficiency

The capacity to actively listen is deemed as one of the utmost crucial attributes for individuals. Individuals experience a sense of solace, empowerment, and value when they are genuinely heard by another individual. When it comes to being a proficient leader, attentive listening enables you to acquire a deeper understanding of the perspectives, viewpoints, and emotions held by others. Each individual possesses their own unique and potentially valuable perspective. When a leader possesses an understanding of the distinctions among their followers, they can utilize such comprehension to assemble a diverse team that collaborates proficiently. Being attentive is valuable when inevitable disagreements arise within the group as well. Exercising leadership, it falls upon you to ensure equity in affording every party an opportunity to articulate their perspective on the matter. These circumstances may elicit strong emotional responses and present challenges in the process of mediation, necessitating a capacity for impartiality and empathetic listening in order to effectively resolve the conflict.

An additional advantageous aspect of possessing proficient listening abilities is the ability to acquire insightful perspectives that may deviate from your own. Initially, achieving the mindset of receptivity towards diverse ideas and opinions can pose as a challenge, however, its value should not be understated. A fundamental aptitude of a proficient listener lies in their capacity to perceive life and the world from another individual's perspective. Individuals possess diverse viewpoints, and it is frequently observed that there exists no singularly correct perspective superior to others. The unique viewpoints held by each individual are of considerable worth and possess the potential to contribute towards generating groundbreaking ideas or making judicious choices, perhaps ones that you would not have conceived independently.

An additional attribute of an effective listener is the consistent upholding of visual engagement. It has been suggested that the primary mode of listening is visual perception, followed by auditory reception. Through visual cues such as eye contact and facial expressions, we engage in extensive nonverbal communication that enables us to discern an individual's emotional condition. Effective eye contact enables individuals to perceive and interpret the unspoken messages conveyed by others. Moreover, it is possible to convey emotions through the use of one's eyes, thereby enabling the individual to comprehend one's understanding of their discourse. Maintaining a vigilant gaze will also demonstrate your sincere engagement with every utterance. Based on one's individual personality disposition, whether characterized as extroverted or introverted, the degree of challenge associated with this attribute of leadership may vary. Active listening holds significant importance in every leadership approach. Even an autocratic leader who wields unfaltering authority can derive advantages from exhibiting attentive listening skills. Individuals who actively engage in attentive listening tend to exhibit heightened powers of observation, thereby enabling them to make optimal and well-informed judgments.

A frequent error individuals commit when engaged in listening is the inclination to draw comparisons between themselves and the other person. This can be problematic. Each individual has their unique perception and interpretation of life's experiences. Please refrain from sharing your personal experience pertaining to their current situation and instead focus on actively listening. It is more advantageous to emphasize the second-person perspective rather than the first-person perspective. The individual engaged in conversation exhibits a lack of genuine interest in your experiences as they prioritize the expression of their own. They are primarily seeking guidance or a compassionate listening ear. It is advisable to discuss how you addressed a situation only when prompted to do so. However, in the event of such a situation, refrain from implying that you have encountered a similar experience as the individual. Please be aware that your experiences may bear resemblance to one another, albeit never identical.

Acquire the skills to show compassion and demonstrate active listening abilities. One could achieve this by occasionally nodding or using affirming sounds such as "mhmm" or any other positive response. Merely gazing into their eyes is frequently insufficient in isolation - one could sustain exceptional visual engagement while their attention is directed elsewhere. Adding other things like, "okay," and "I see," along with the eye contact will show even more that you are truly listening. However, it is imperative to strategically incorporate those words or phrases during opportune moments, as one must exercise caution to avoid inadvertently uttering inappropriate remarks or seeming excessively interruptive.

Throughout every conversation, make sure to meticulously record all the essential aspects of the individual's discourse. Reiterating previously mentioned points during the process of providing feedback demonstrates attentive listening, thus fostering a desire within the individual to share further information. It is not mandatory for you to retain the exact words uttered by the individual; it suffices to make a mental note of one essential aspect discussed within a five-minute interval. By engaging in this practice, you can maintain ongoing communication with the individual, even long after the initial conversation has concluded. Exercising the skill of timely follow-up is equally vital for an effective leader.

The ultimate aspect to refine your listening skills is to possess the knowledge of what to articulate and the appropriate timing to do so. Please refrain from attempting to communicate prematurely, as it is essential to engage in attentive listening prior to expressing your thoughts. There may be instances wherein the need to vocalize one's thoughts or opinions is not necessary. In instances where an individual discloses something of an emotional and personal nature, it is incumbent upon one to adopt a sympathetic demeanor and offer reassurance with respect to maintaining the utmost confidentiality. An effective listener is also someone who demonstrates discretion when necessary. In the event that it is deemed suitable to express opinions or provide feedback once the individual has concluded their discourse, make an effort to recollect and reiterate all the primary facets of the conversation, incorporating your perspectives or evaluations on each facet.

Personal Health

The definition of health according to the World Health Organization examines personal well-being through three distinct lenses: Physical, Mental, and Spiritual. Presented here is a succinct summary of each individual item.

Physical Health

Your objective is to attain a state of physical well-being. Several circumstances lie beyond your influence, including genetic anomalies, physical traumas, and specific illnesses. Nevertheless, there remains the potential to enhance your individual well-being by means of the decisions you undertake. For instance, let us contemplate the well-being of your dental structures, including both teeth and gums, which are susceptible to deterioration based on your oral care practices. To our great advantage, the groundbreaking efforts carried out by the National Human Genome Research Institute have bestowed upon us the capacity to discern specific detrimental genes, enabling us to embrace preventive measures aimed at mitigating their influence on our well-being.

One ill-advised decision has the potential to have long-lasting consequences for various aspects of your wellbeing over the course of your life. However, oftentimes, your health behaviors are shaped by repeated choices, which establish ingrained habits in your health-related practices. These involuntary decisions may encompass aspects such as dietary patterns and nutritional habits, the nature and extent of physical exertion or alternative forms of exercise, as well as the selection of companions and companionships. Participation in social networks can influence behaviors such as tobacco consumption, alcohol intake, substance abuse, or dietary habits. All of them exert influence on your overall state of welfare.

www.ingramcontent.com/pod-product-compliance
Lightning Source LLC
Chambersburg PA
CBHW052147110526
44591CB00012B/1886